Gold Medal Advisory Board

OLYMPIC BOBSLEDDING

By the staff of the Ice Skating Institute of America
in cooperation with the United States Olympic Committee

CHILDRENS PRESS, CHICAGO

Left and opposite:
The United States
four-man bobsled
team in 1972, Sapporo.

Photographs in this book courtesy of the Ice Skating Institute of America, publisher, *XIII Olympic Winter Games, Lake Placid,* © 1979.
Created by T.A. Chacharon & Assoc. Ltd.
Cover photograph: The West German gold-medal bobsled team, 1972.
Page 1 photograph: The United States bobsled team, 1976.

LIBRARY OF CONGRESS CATALOGING IN PUBLICATION DATA

Ice Skating Institute of America.
  Olympic bobsledding.

  SUMMARY: Describes the origins, equipment, techniques, and events
of Olympic bobsledding and tobogganing with emphasis on the achievements
of several Olympic champions.
  1. Bobsledding—History—Juvenile literature. 2. Tobogganing—
History—Juvenile literature. 3. Olympic games—Juvenile literature.
[1. Bobsledding. 2. Tobogganing. 3. Olympic games (winter)]
I. United States Olympic Committee. II. Title.
GV856.I24   1979   796.9'5   79-18842
ISBN 0-516-02552-X

You stand quietly with your partner, counting to yourself as you prepare for your run down the slope. The test has finally come. All of your preparation and your work together will end in victory or defeat.

Your bobsled is at the starting point. You tell the starter you are ready. Your hand grasps the handles of the sled. The starter shouts, "Go!" You push with all your might and jump into the running sled. The race has begun.

Your bob begins to pick up speed. You enter the first turn, body weight shifting, timed perfectly with your partner. The bob makes the turn with a precise move. You work on turn after turn, each one perfectly timed, each perfect turn bringing you closer to victory.

You can feel the wind whistling past your face. All around you are white walls. You almost do not need to see the course ahead of you. You have made this run before with your partner, and every bump and curve is burned into your brain.

Three more turns to go. Done! Now the next. Perfect! The last curve comes — and then you are flashing past the finish line. Your run has ended. When your score is put up on the scoreboard, you whoop and smile. You have won a gold medal!

5

*The 1956 Swiss Olympic team zooms
past a timer on a dangerous curve.*

Anyone who has ever belly flopped down a hill on a sled has an idea of what bobsledding is like. But he has had only a taste of the thrill and danger. Few sports are faster, more dangerous, or more exciting than flashing down an icy incline at speeds that sometimes approach 90 miles an hour. Participants and spectators from all over the world eagerly await, take part in, and watch these spectacular races. People in open machines are rushing down an ice tunnel, with only their skill and daring to keep them from flying off the course! The irresistable combination of speed and danger makes bobsledding and luge tobogganing among the most popular of the Winter Olympic events.

HOW SLED RACING BEGAN

The sled is even older than the wheel as a means of moving things over some distance. Cave drawings from fifteen thousand years ago show that people used sleds over dry ground as well as over snow-covered ground. After the wheel was invented, the sled was used only in the winter. Animals were often hitched to the sleds to help in hauling food and other supplies. Sleds constructed from skins and bones were used by Eskimos. American Indians invented wooden sleds with turned-up front ends. They called them toboggans. Messengers of the Roman army used sleds for moving swiftly from mountains to camps. People in the Alps of Europe used them for delivering mail and getting across the mountains quickly.

7

The United States team of Curtis and Hubert Stevens heat their bobsled runners before winning the gold medal in 1932.

Sleds were used only as a means of transportation for thousands of years. In the 1500s people began to discover what fun it could be to whoosh down a mountain on a sled. But sledding was not turned into a sport until the middle of the 1800s. Until then, people had to do almost everything by hand. In the 1800s machines were invented that could do some of the work formerly done by human beings. Many people suddenly had more time for leisure activities. Vacationers who wanted to have fun turned sledding into a racing event.

The popularity of sledding, or tobogganing as it was known then, grew rapidly. The first course designed for toboggan racing was built in 1879, and the first official international race for toboggans was held in 1883. Different kinds of sleds were developed. On some, the rider lay on his or her stomach and guided the sled. On others, the rider lay on his or her back or sat upright. *Bobsledding* came into being when two sleds were joined together by a board. *Luge tobogganing* was done on a single sled; the rider lay on his or her back.

The bobsled became the most popular of the racing sleds. Its design was gradually changed until it looked something like a small car with no roof or trunk, and with two sets of runners instead of wheels. The first time bobsledding was held as part of the Winter Olympic Games was in 1924. It was a four-man bobsled event. Racing for two-man bobsleds became part of the Olympics in 1932.

Because bobsledding was so popular, the luge toboggan with its single set of runners was ignored for a time. It grew more popular in the 1930s and 1940s. A change in its design had made it more flexible

This picture shows a modern bobsled. The small hood,
or cowl, in the front is designed to cut down wind
resistance. The sled is steered by a steering wheel.
The serrated brake is located between the back runners.

and just as exciting to watch as bobsledding. In the 1950s it was decided by the International Olympic Committee (IOC) that luge be admitted as another Winter Olympic event. In 1960 there was no bobsledding event at the Games, so it was not until 1964 that luge tobogganing made its first appearance in the Olympics. While bobsledding was a men-only event, the luge event was open to both male and female competitors. Bobsledding and luge became two of the most popular events for spectators. The spectacle of people whizzing down an icy run at high speed is hard to beat.

THE BOBSLED AND ITS TEAM

The modern bobsled is very different from the crude wooden sleds used by early peoples. It is made of steel and aluminum. The front of the bob has a small hood, or *cowl,* covering it. This cowl is designed to cut down wind resistance. The back of the bob is open. There are seats in the open section for either two or four men. Handles on the sled are used to move it at the start of the race. Underneath the sled are two pairs of *runners.* The front runners are movable. They are steered either by ropes or by a steering wheel. The runners in the back are bolted to the sled so that they are fixed in place. Between the back runners is the *brake.* The brake is a very hard piece of steel. It has a sharp, serrated edge, much like the edge of a steak knife. When the brake is applied, this edge cuts deeply into the ice. Because the brake does cut

11

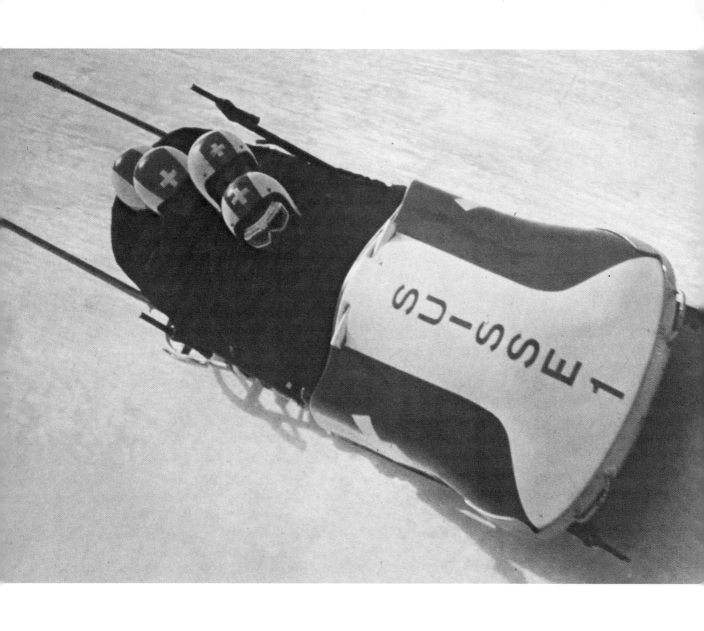

so deeply, it may not be used during the run to control the bobsled. If it were used, it might ruin the surface of the run and make it dangerous for the other bobsledders. Only in an emergency may the brakeman apply the brake while on the run.

The weight of the bobsled and its riders is carefully controlled. In early bobsled competitions only the sled itself was weighed. Teams whose members weighed a lot had an advantage over lighter teams. The heavier teams moved faster down the course. In modern competitions the bobsled and its team members are weighed together. The most a two-man sled with its riders may weigh is 827 pounds. A four-man bob and its team may weigh 1,389 pounds. If a team is under these allowed weights, metal weights may be added to their sled to bring them to the maximum limit. With all bobsleds weighing the same, the competition is fairer.

A two-man sled, sometimes called a *boblet,* may be up to 8 feet, 10 inches long. It may not be more than 2 feet, 2¼ inches wide, and its seats may not be more than 8 inches off the ground. The four-man bob has the same width and seat requirements, but it may be up to 12 feet, 5 inches long. These long, low sleds of specific sizes also help make the competition more equal. With the weight and the size controlled, the skill of each team decides the winner.

13

*Even back in 1936 this United States four-man
bobsled team wore safety helmets for protection.*

All bobsled team members must wear crash helmets for safety. The sleds sometimes go 90 miles an hour. If a sled tipped over during a run, team members without helmets could be seriously hurt. The team members also wear goggles to cut down the glare from the icy course and to keep the wind out of their eyes. Padding on their knees and elbows helps keep them from getting hurt during a spill.

The bobsledders must be a team in every sense of the word. They must perform as if they were one man. The way a team starts a race often decides how well the team will do on the run. The initial "heave" the team gives the sled helps its speed. On the course the team members must also work together. Each member must lean his weight to the right or left at the same moment to help the bob go around curves. They must also center their weight at the same time when coming out of a curve. If even one team member does not perform with the others, the bobsled could be thrown off balance. The team might lose precious seconds, and it could cost them a race.

BOBSLED COMPETITION

In the Olympics there are two parts to the bobsled competition, the *two-man bob* and the *four-man bob*. Each team races its bobsled four times down a specially constructed course. The teams run two races, or *heats,* for two days in a row. The times of the four runs are added together, and the team with the lowest score is the winner.

*The 1976 United States Olympic four-man
bobsled team is off to a flying start.*

For the Olympics, the bobsled course must be at least 1,500 meters long. There are usually about fifteen curves on the course. The course looks something like a tunnel that snakes sharply down a mountain. Many bobsled courses are made artificially. They have a base of stone or concrete. Snow and ice are frozen onto this base to make a solid wall of ice. On each of the curves the walls of the course are much higher than on the straight sections. The walls at the curves are sometimes 20 feet tall. These banked walls keep the speeding bobsled from shooting off the course when there is a sharp curve.

Before the Olympics, all teams that plan to compete in the Games are required to train on the course they will be using for the races. This practice helps each team compete as safely as possible. Two-man teams train for five days before the competitions, and four-man teams for four days. They must know the course thoroughly. Teams that do not train for the required number of days may not be allowed to enter the contests.

The teams draw numbers to determine their starting order. When the races are about to begin, they line up in that order. Each team starts the race with a *flying start* or a *standing start*. Each member of the team stands beside his bobsled. The starter asks the team captain if he is ready. When the captain says "Yes," the starter says, "Attention! Go!" The team members either run with their bobsled for a few meters and hop on when it gains speed, or push it a few steps and then jump on the moving bob.

William Fiske, pilot of the 1932 four-man
gold-medal bobsled team at Lake Placid, New York,
is presented the world championship trophy.

When the bobsled crosses the starting line, electronic timing of the run begins. The captain of the team steers the bobsled around the curves of the run. The brakeman, at the back of the bob, keeps the sled from skidding and brings it to a halt when the race is finished. On a four-man bobsled, there are also two team members between the captain and the brakeman. Their body weight is important in keeping the sled from flying off the track on curves. All members of a team must shift their weight at the proper time so that they do not lose a fraction of a second while going down the run. When the bobsled breaks an electronic beam at the end of the run, the clock is stopped.

FAMOUS BOBSLEDDERS

Although bobsledding is a team sport, it is the drivers of the bobs who earn fame. The driver is the head of the team. His skill in picking out the best route over the icy course greatly affects the outcome of the race.

Early Olympic champions were often from the United States or Switzerland. **William Fiske** was one of the brightest United States bobsledders. He piloted his four-man bobs to gold medals in the 1928 and 1932 Winter Games. He piloted something else, too—airplanes. His daring and love of speed had led him to a career in aviation. Fiske lost his life in an air crash in 1941.

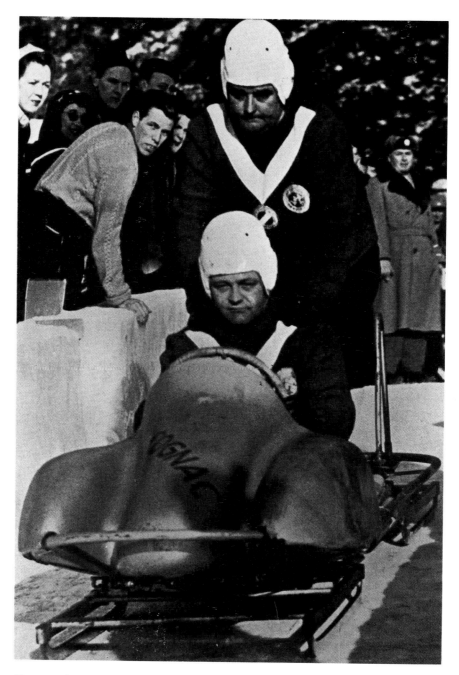

*Germany's two-man bobsled (boblet) team,
Andreas Ostler, captain, and Lorenz Nieberl,
brakeman, won the gold in 1952. This
team, much heavier than most other
competitors, had a definite advantage in
the event. For the following Olympic
bobsledding competitions, weight rules were added.*

Swiss stars included **Hanns Kilian,** a three-time world champion, and **Fritz Feierabend,** who designed many of the bobsleds used in the 1950s. Feierabend had had a nineteen-year career in bobsledding before he turned to designing bobs.

In the 1948 Winter Games at St. Moritz, Switzerland the United States won its last gold medal to date. **Francis Tyler** won the four-man event, while Swiss great **Felix Endrich** took the honors in the two-man bob. **Frederick Fortune,** also of the United States, won the bronze medal in the two-man event. His was a remarkable career. He was active in bobsledding for twenty-two seasons, and drove his last races in 1969.

The domination of the United States and Switzerland ended with the 1952 Olympics, when **Andreas Ostler** of Germany captained both the two-man and four-man sleds and won both gold medals. Ostler and his teammates, who were much heavier than most of the other competitors, had an advantage over the lighter competitors. After the 1952 Games, weight rules were added to the bobsledding competition. In those same games **Stanley Benham** of the United States took silver medals in both events. He and his team had held the world championship for the four-man bobsled for the two years before the 1952 competitions.

For the next Games—in 1956 at Cortina, Italy—the Swiss produced another winner in **Franz Kapus,** who took the gold in the four-man event. Kapus was forty-seven years old that year, the oldest person ever to win a Winter Olympic gold medal. Bobsledding had become

Eugenio Monti's four-man Italian team took a silver medal in the 1956 Olympics at Cortina, Italy. Monti also captained the two-man bobsled team to a silver medal that year.

very popular in Italy, and two Italians walked off with honors. **Lamberto Dalla Costa** won a gold medal in the two-man race, and **Eugenio Monti** took silver medals in both events. Monti, then twenty-eight years old, was destined to become probably the most famous bobsledder of all time. He did not get a crack at another Olympic championship until 1964. Bobsledding competitions were not held in the 1960 Games at Squaw Valley, California because the Olympic Committee decided that it would be too expensive to construct a bobsled course.

In 1964, Innsbruck, Austria was the setting of one of the most interesting bobsled competitions ever held. **Victor Emery** of Canada guided his four-man bob to a first-place finish. United States coach Stanley Benham called it the "biggest upset in bobsledding history"—with good reason. In 1964 there wasn't a bobsled in all of Canada. Emery and his team had almost no experience in bobsledding, but won the Olympic gold as well as the world championship in 1964. It marked Canada's first gold medal in bobsledding.

The two-man races were equally dramatic. **Eugenio Monti** was pitted against **Tony Nash,** a British bobsledding star. Monti was leading going into the fourth and last run of the competition. He had finished his run and was waiting to see how Nash would do. Suddenly Nash's voice came over the loudspeaker, asking for help. A bolt that held his runners to his sled had snapped, and he needed another to make his run. Monti ran to his sled, took his own bolt out, and sent it up the course for Nash to use. Nash made his run, and won the gold medal.

23

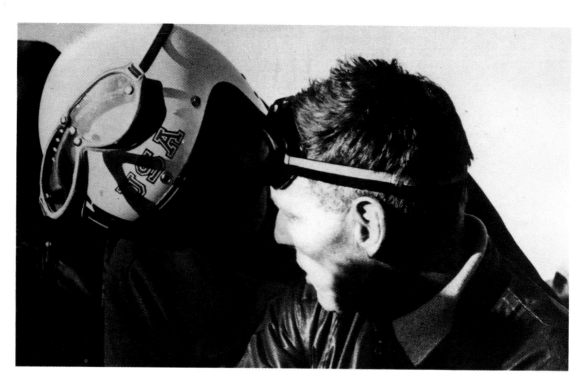

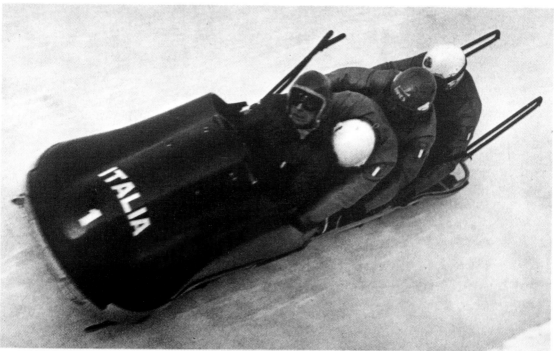

Through his unselfish act, Monti had lost the gold medal, but he had shown a true Olympic spirit.

Monti, however, was not finished yet in Olympic competition. While Nash became involved in technical improvements in bobsleds, Monti had one more try in the 1968 Games at Grenoble, France. In that year Monti was forty years old. He had won eight world championships, five in two-man events and three in four-man events. He finished his career by taking both gold medals in the 1968 Olympics. It was a near thing in the two-man event. His closest rival was **Horst Floth** of West Germany. When the times of their runs were added, they had matched each other to the hundredth of a second! The judges were not sure just what to do. Then someone remembered a rule that stated that the winner of the first heat would take the championship in case of a tie. Monti had won that heat, and happily received his gold medal.

The four-man victory was also exciting. Because the weather was turning warmer and threatened to soften the track, the judges decided the race on only two runs instead of the four that were ordinarily required. Monti again won. His twelve-year wait for the Olympic honors had been rewarded. Monti retired after the 1968 Games and became the coach of the Italian teams.

25

*Opposite: A West German two-man bobsled team sweeps down
a straightaway at the Sapporo, Japan Olympics in 1972.*

The Sapporo, Japan Games of 1972 ended in victory for West German bobsledders. **Wolfgang Zimmerer,** in a two-man bob, led the field in run after run to win the gold medal. The fight for the other medals was very exciting. **Horst Floth,** the man who had lost to Monti in the 1968 Olympics, put forth a great effort in his last run and won another silver medal. He pushed **Jean Wicki** of Switzerland back to third place. But Wicki would not be denied a victory, and led his team to a gold medal in the four-man competition.

In 1976, Innsbruck, Austria was the scene for the debut of East Germany's bobsledding team. After long preparation and only a year in international competition, the East Germans won victories in both events. Both winning bobs were headed by **Meinhard Nehmer,** a stern-faced thirty-five-year-old army staff sergeant. Nehmer became the third person to win double medals in Olympic bobsledding competition.

THE LUGE AND ITS COURSE

A luge toboggan looks much like the sled used by children in the winter. It has a wooden frame with sharpened metal runners. The tobogganer sits on a seat of woven fabric strips. He or she holds a hand rope attached to the frame, while the other hand holds on to the wooden frame. The runners curve up slightly beyond the wooden frame. To steer, the tobogganer moves the runners by pushing against

27

them with his or her feet. The luge is controlled by the pushing of the runners and the shifting of body weight. No brakes are permitted on luge toboggans.

Luges are very lightweight and small. A single-seater luge may weigh only forty-four pounds; the double-seater is only two or three pounds heavier. The runners may be no more than 1 foot, 5⅜ inches apart. The height of the entire toboggan may be anywhere between 4¾ inches and 5⅞ inches above the ground. The standard size and weight of the luges ensure that competitors' skills are being tested and not the design of their sleds.

The luge course looks like a bobsled run, but there are many more curves in it and it has a steeper descent. The specially built courses are always artificial. In some competitions, luge racers use the bobsled runs that have already been built. This was the case in the 1976 Winter Games at Innsbruck, Austria. The luge course is shorter than the bobsled run. It ranges from 1,000 to 1,500 meters. There are two starting areas on a luge course. The women's and pair's events run over only four-fifths of the course, while the men's individual event covers the entire distance. Many courses are lit by spotlights so that the event can be held at night when it is colder and the ice stays frozen more easily. Many of the courses are refrigerated so that the ice will be hard, especially on the many curves.

29

Kathleen Homstad of the United States takes her luge around a hairpin turn at sixty miles per hour. She is steering the toboggan by pushing against the runners with her feet.

OLYMPIC COMPETITION

Three luge events are held in the Olympics: *men's individual, women's individual,* and *pair's races.* All those who compete in the races are required to go through intensive training on the course they will be using during the Olympic competition. First the tobogganers are taken on a slow tour of the course. They inspect the curves and their placement so that there will be no surprises when they start their runs. They may take short runs down the course, starting near the end or in the middle, so that they can get the feel of the course. Finally they are allowed to run the whole length of the course. The tobogganers should try to get in four runs on the course, including one at night. They *must* make at least two non-stop runs of the entire course.

The luge tobogganers in each event draw for their starting order, and then line up in that order before each race, or heat. Each competitor in turn starts the run from a sitting position on the luge. They are warned by the race starter that they will start by a countdown. Ten seconds before the racer must shoot down the run, the starter says, "Get ready—get set—go!" The tobogganer then pushes off down the course, and his or her timing begins.

The racers guide their toboggans down the slope as quickly as they can. They steer their luges with feet pressing down on each of the runners, by pulling on the hand rope, and by shifting their weight from one runner to the other. At one time racers sat upright as they went

31

down a course. Today's racers lean back as far as possible so that the wind created on their run does not slow them down. If the tobogganers need to control their speed on a straight part of the course, they can sit upright to slow themselves down.

When a luge goes by the finish line, the clock is stopped. Each person or pair makes four runs down the course during the Games. Their times are added together, and the winning toboggan is the one with the lowest time.

Olympic luge racers may be penalized in several ways. They may be disqualified if they fail to wear crash helmets. They may not warm up the runners of their toboggans to make them go faster. Weights may not be attached to luge racers' clothes or to the toboggans to make them heavier than the weight allowed. No one may help the racers push off at the starting point. The racers may receive help on the course only if it is impossible for them to get the toboggan to move. The racers must always be aware of safety, and may not act in a dangerous manner during a race. Any racer who does not follow the rules may have a particular run disqualified or may be removed from the competition entirely.

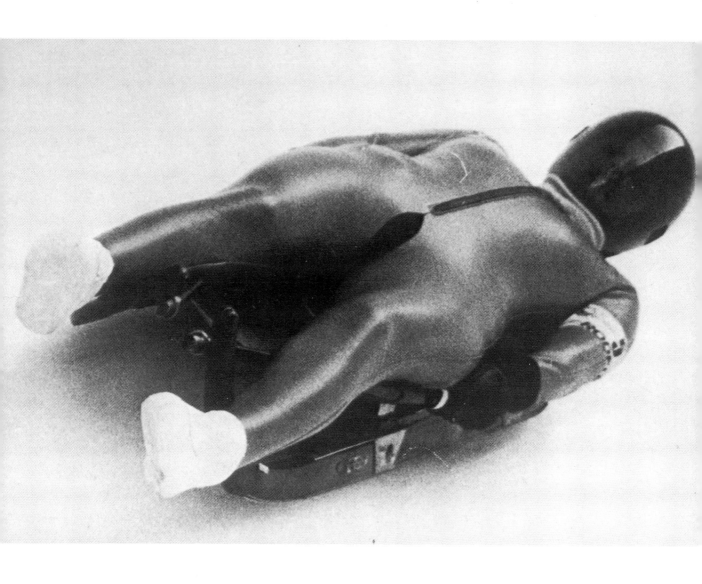

OLYMPIC LUGE CHAMPIONS

Luge tobogganing was first held as part of the Innsbruck, Austria Winter Games in 1964. From the start, East Germans seem to have dominated the event. **Thomas Koehler,** a three-time world champion, beat his teammate **Klaus Bonsack** by three-tenths of a second to win the gold medal in the men's individual competition. In the women's individual event the "queen of tobogganers," **Ortrun Enderlein,** posted the fastest runs and also took a gold. The only gold medal the East Germans failed to take was for the men's pairs competition. That honor went to **Josef Feistmantl** and **Manfred Stengl** of Austria. In that same year, Feistmantl and Stengl went on from the Olympics to win the world championship pairs event.

The 1968 Winter Games at Grenoble, France were filled with problems. The luge competition was almost canceled because not enough countries had entered teams. At least twelve countries must participate in an Olympic event. Finally, enough nations were willing to put up teams for the luge event. Then the weather warmed up while the contestants were practicing on the runs. Everyone was afraid that the luge course would not be hard enough for the races. The weather finally turned cold enough and the races were held.

35

Vera Zozulia of the U.S.S.R.
at Innsbruck, Austria in 1976.

Angelika Schafferer of Austria checks her equipment before racing in 1976.

A third problem developed during the women's competition. One of the judges found out that the East Germans were heating up their luge runners before making their runs. This is illegal in luge competitions. The three East German women were winning when this was discovered. They were disqualified from the Olympics. Among the disqualified women was **Ortrun Enderlein,** the former Olympic gold medalist. With the top two women out of the running, **Erica Lechner** of Italy won the top prize in the women's competition. In the men's individual event the winner was **Manfred Schmid** from Austria. East Germany recovered a bit in the pairs competition. **Thomas Koehler** and **Klaus Bonsack,** who had finished first and second in the 1964 men's individual event, teamed up to win the gold medal in the 1968 pairs competition.

Opposite: Wolfgang Scheidel of East Germany won the gold medal for men's singles luge in 1972.

In 1972 East German tobogganers again made almost a clean sweep of the top medals. Their teams took all but one of the nine medals offered in the luge competitions. Leading the teams were gold medalists **Wolfgang Scheidel** in the men's individual event, **Anna Marie Mueller** in the women's individual event, and the duo of **Horst Hornlein** and **Reinhard Bradow** in the men's pairs. Hornlein and Bradow were not alone, however. The Italian team of **Paul Hildgartner** and **Walter Plainkner** matched their times, and so shared the gold medal with the East German team.

At Innsbruck, Austria in 1976, luge became even more exciting to watch. The riders had improved their sleds so that they could make even faster times. They also wore helmets that were egg-shaped or pointed to cut down the wind resistance. Once more spectators saw East German riders triumph. Only West Germany and Austria produced riders capable of meeting the East German challenge. This year the top medalists were **Peter Guenther** in the men's individual event, **Margit Schumann** in the women's individual event, and the team of **Hans Rinn** and **Norbert Hahn** in the pairs.

Opposite: West Germany came in third in the four-man bobsled race in 1976.

Below: Italy's four-man team came in with a silver medal in 1976.

Opposite: The United States' four-man bobsled team received a silver medal in 1952.

Below: Germany won the gold medal in 1952 with Andreas Ostler steering to victory.

*Japan's two-man team takes a sharp
curve in the 1976 Olympics.*

An old photograph of a four man bobsled team taking a curve in 1936.

OLYMPIC GOLD MEDALISTS
Bobsledding

TWO MAN

Year	Country
1932	United States I
1936	United States I
1948	Switzerland II
1952	Germany I
1956	Italy I
1960	Event not on program
1964	Great Britain
1968	Italy
1972	West Germany
1976	East Germany I

FOUR MAN

Year	Country
1924	Switzerland I
1928	United States II
1932	United States I
1936	Switzerland II
1948	United States II
1952	Germany
1956	Switzerland I
1960	Event not on program
1964	Canada I
1968	Italy I
1972	Switzerland
1976	East Germany

47

OLYMPIC GOLD MEDALISTS
Tobagganing (Luge)

SINGLE SEATER
MEN

Year	Name	Country
1964	Thomas Koehler	Germany
1968	Manfred Schmid	Austria
1972	Wolfgang Scheidel	East Germany
1976	Detlef Guenther	East Germany

SINGLE SEATER
WOMAN

Year	Name	Country
1964	Otrum Enderlein	Germany
1968	Erica Lechner	Italy
1972	Anna Marie Muller	East Germany
1976	Margit Schumann	East Germany

TWO SEATER
MEN

Year	Name	Country
1964		Austria
1968		East Germany
1972	Paul Hildgartner, Walter Plaikner	Italy
1972	Horst Hornlein, Reinhard Bredow	East Germany
1976	Hans Rinn, Norbert Hahn	East Germany